SERVANT LEADERSHIP

Danny Doucette

Copyright© 2020

All rights reserved

All rights to this book are reserved. No permission is given for any part of this book to be reproduced, transmitted in any form or means; electronic or mechanical, stored in a retrieval system, photocopied, recorded, scanned, or otherwise. Any of these actions require the proper written permission of the publisher.

Table of Contents

DISCLAIMER 1

INTRODUCTION 3

CHAPTER 1: WHAT SERVANT LEADERSHIP LOOKS LIKE 5

CHAPTER 2: POSITIONAL SERVANT 37

CHAPTER 3: TIMES ARE CHANGING IN TERMS OF LEADERSHIP QUALITY AND STANDARD 49

CHAPTER 4: BECOMING A SERVANT LEADER 63

CONCLUSION 83

ABOUT THE AUTHOR 85

Disclaimer

All knowledge contained in this book is given for informational and educational purposes only. The author is not in any way accountable for any results or outcomes that emanate from using this material. Constructive attempts have been made to provide information that is both accurate and effective, but the author is not bound for the accuracy or use/misuse of this information.

Introduction

Do you know that the greatest success that can be achieved by a leader is to have the support of those he leads? Followers tend to dote on leaders who have their interest at heart, and there are not many leaders out there who have been able to achieve this attainable feat. This inability to influence followers is because the secret(s) to successful leadership is not known by many, especially those who lead based on the powers of their position. Knowing these secrets can help you transcend your present predicaments of not being able to influence your followers positively.

Many scholars in past centuries have stated that leaders who tend to put their subjects ahead of every other thing tend to get more loyalty than others. But of particular interest is the recent development of servant leadership proposed and practiced by Robert K. Greenleaf in 1970[1]. Greenleaf is known for his impact

---

1 https://en.wikipedia.org/wiki/Robert_K._Greenleaf

on the growth and development of potential leaders who can pique the interest of their followers.

Although many leaders might not realize it, their inability to influence their followers results from them focusing their leadership on themselves. Servant leadership provides excellent insight on how to bridge this gap between followers and leaders by bringing leadership closer to the people. People tend to flourish better when they are led under the principles of servant leadership, and so do the leader and the community in general flourish.

This book explores the processes of moving you towards becoming a servant leader in 12 months. These are not just ordinary steps that would leave you bereft of greater development as a leader open to learning. Check to see the changes that would occur in your leadership traits and characteristics and see a positive difference. If there are no changes, then this book is not for you!

Chapter One
WHAT SERVANT LEADERSHIP LOOKS LIKE

Servant leadership has always existed as an approach used by exemplary leaders for centuries to lead their followers to greater heights. So many leadership successes are attributed to those leaders who have employed this approach, putting their followers first in all actions and inactions. However, the concept of "servant leadership" is relatively new to our world today. Robert K. Greenleaf first coined "servant leadership" in his essay, "The Servant as a Leader[2]," written in 1970.

What, then, is servant leadership? According to Greenleaf, servant leadership is when the "Servant-leader is servant first, it begins with a natural feeling that one wants to serve, to serve first, as opposed to wanting power, influence, fame, or wealth[3]." This set of practice is a philosophy that can be a driving force

2 https://www.greenleaf.org/what-is-servant-leadership/
3 https://www.goodreads.com/author/quotes/105978.Robert_K_Greenleaf

that holds the potential to develop and gear individuals, organizations, and the world towards success.

The consideration of servant-leader is always to put the interests and needs of members of one's team or community first, depending on those one lead. It is after every other person has been placed first into consideration that the servant-leader thinks of himself.

Acknowledging the importance of others, their opinions, their goals, a sense of collectivity, and giving them necessary support at all times is a sure-fire way to trigger success. Why? Because people tend to engage more, commit themselves, and build stronger relationships amongst themselves when placed as a priority.

With the implementation of servant leadership comes the displacement of the usual air of authority and benefits that a leader enjoys. A leader here is not concerned about exerting the apparent powers of their office, but to lead others selflessly. It is this exemplary attitude that every selfless servant leader takes in dispensing with their duties and obligations.

The aim of servant leadership is, therefore, to empower your team members to grow and be happy with themselves. They feel an immediate sense of purpose when their needs are placed above that of the leader himself. This can lead to significant total commitment, enthusiasm, and desire to deliver the expectations or targets of the organization. This feeling ultimately leads to the delivery of quality service, satisfaction, and happiness of customers.

Servant leadership does not come ordinarily to everyone. With being a servant leader comes that conscientiousness that one wants to serve others, that is, leading by putting others first. It is this conscientious feeling that guides one to have original thoughts of leading others.

Servant leaders often try their all to help those who struggle around them, and those who are doing better are propelled to do much better than they do. By contrast, such quality or feeling is lost and not found in someone who puts their position as a leader ahead of other people. The way a leader who serves first leads will differ from one who leads first.

While this chapter does not intend to explain in detail the difference(s) between the servant leader and the leader who leads first, it won't hurt to check out some intricate differences. The main difference that prevails between the two leading human leadership positions is who and what is prioritized first. The servant-leader places much esteem and priority on the needs of those he leads. Such a leader is more concerned about the fulfillment of the development of those who see him as their leader. It is this focus on the benefits, growths, and goals of those around him that leads to success. Those who follow such a leader readily give their all towards achieving set-out tasks within the corporation or organization.

On the other hand, a traditional leader who puts leading first of others is likely to exercise power by being the leader. The focus of growth and development within the organization or corporation is driven by the mere desires of the leader alone. These stand out as the difference between the two. In chapter 2 of this book, we would discuss in detail what differences exist between the two leadership positions.

Effects of servant leadership

Although there are both negative and positive effects stemming from establishing a servant leadership position, the positives far outweigh the negatives. As we will see, several notes can be derived from using the servant leadership profile to lead one's followers.

Positives of engaging in a servant leadership profile

There are some interesting, positive high points of maintaining or adopting a servant leadership style. Every business or organizational model has some benefits it could enjoy from using this leadership style philosophy to grow and develop its business. Here are a few notes to take on the benefits of servant leadership.

The mutual benefit of all is made a priority in decision making

The major highlight of servant leadership is that the consideration of every other individual or team member is prioritized in an organization's decision making. The realization here is that for the goals of the corporation or organization to be realized, the role of those working within is of importance. Everyone is then given an equal opportunity to contribute to the decision-making process.

Treating everyone right by recognizing their overall value and contributions to the organization is paramount here. It will help to reach individual and organizational targets or goals. Hence, the need to place value on the interests of everyone on the team, right from the members at the bottom of the organization to the top. Greenleaf highlights this important point when he says, "The best leaders are clear. They continually light the way, and in the process, let each person know that what they do makes a difference. The best test as a leader is: Do those served grow as persons; do they become healthier, wiser, freer, more autonomous, more likely themselves to become leaders[4]?"

Personal and organizational growth is encouraged

The friendly, conductive environment where everybody has some value and prestige given to him or her has a way of encouraging growth and development. Despite the realization

4 https://www.azquotes.com/quote/648249

that everyone has different talents, responsibilities, and roles brought to the table, everyone is made to work for the mutual benefit of all. Joe Paterno, the famous Penn State football coach says, "when a team outgrows individual performance and learns team confidence, excellence becomes a reality.[5]" Such an environment allows those who have difficulties, expertise, and strengths in different areas to help grow and develop together as one. The diversity here is employed to drive everyone towards the same destination- achieving set-out goals. This conducive environment can lead to an enormous surge in the accomplishment of the organization's setout goals and targets.

Empathy is encouraged

Have you ever considered what the result of a leader who makes decisions based on placing themselves in the shoes of others would be? It would inevitably lead to striking out decisions and reasons that don't tend to benefit others. A leader in this situation will easily refuse to do the bidding of others that don't follow up in line with general consideration. The leader realizes here that what is best for the business is to consider the business and team members in one piece. Robert Greenleaf says, "Servant leadership always empathizes, always accepts the person, but sometimes refuses to accept some of the person's effort or performance as good enough[6]."

---

5 https://www.biography.com/news/joe-paterno-movie-hbo-paterno
6 https://www.azquotes.com/author/19554-Robert_K_Greenleaf

Customer interest is served better

Customers of an organization tend to be served in the best possible way as a consequence of a leader serving their team members. By placing value on members of the organization's interests above their own, the leader has planted a seed of service in their team. Taking a cue from their leader, team members devote themselves to their customers, offering them constant support, better services, and care. The employees are more confident and enthusiastic, dispensing their duties and functions to their customers based on the vote of a confidence reposed on them by their leader. With this, the organization stands a higher chance of growing and developing exponentially. James Hunter has the same points when he says, "To have a healthy and thriving business, there must be healthy relationships with the C.E.O.S. in the organization and I'm not referring to the Chief Executive Officers. I am talking about the Customers, the Employees, the Owner (or stockholders), and the Suppliers[7]."

The focus is on achieving obtainable goals and results

What is of concern to a leader or manager in every situation in organizational planning is obtaining favorable results. The goal here is neither to achieve personal or egoistic desires, nor is it to express one's own glory of being the brain behind organizational success. These successes do not fall into the

---

7 https://www.azquotes.com/quote/1035197

consideration of a leader while he makes decisions to grow and develop the organization.

Potentials, creativity, and a sense of purpose are unlocked

The mindset of serving people first comes with that passion for always empowering and uplifting members of the team. The feeling of being in command and an air of authority is dropped for humility before employees. The leader here looks to align the sense of purpose of workers with the goals of the organization. The result of this is just as you think it is. The results here go out through the roof, way beyond reasonable comprehension, growing and developing an organization's goals exponentially.

Bill Hybel says, "Coaching is the most important servant/leadership element in helping people accomplish their goals[8]." Every servant leader must then face this task squarely. It is their responsibility that their employees harness their potentials and talents through their tutelage, encouragement, and guidance.

The happiness of the leader is guaranteed

Servant leaders tend to feel gladdened when they are aware of their level of success leading people who are happy and successful. It is itself an accomplishment for them as they look forward to the prospect of coming back to work or within the

---

8 https://developingsuperleaders.wordpress.com/2018/01/24/coaching-is-the-most-important-servant-leadership-element-in-helping-people-accomplish-their-goals-bill-hybels/

society to teach people to serve others. Albert Schweitzer says, "I don't know what your destiny will be, but one thing I know: the only ones among you who will be really happy are those who will have sought and found how to serve[9]." This quotation indicates the excitement a leader who serves gets when he makes it happen each day at their place of work or in the society.

The tone or path for an organization's success is set

Servant leadership encourages team members to share their interests, ideas, and thoughts over time of how best to move the organization forward. There is no anxiety whatsoever from the employees of being put down by the boss for making useful suggestions. Employees seeing the encouragement their leader gives to sharing ideas are easily spurred to think beyond the box. They are propelled to think beyond the present realities of the organization to what can better the current conditions of work.

Negatives of engaging in a servant leadership profile

We have seen how employing servant leadership can be of benefit to its users, both team members and their leaders. However, there are some important negative aspects of the use of the leadership style in an establishment. Here are some of the critical disadvantages of servant leadership.

---

9 https://www.brainyquote.com/quotes/albert_schweitzer_133001

Decision making tends to take longer than usual

The process of making decisive decisions for an organization's growth could be slowed down from having to consider everyone. Unlike having to take a direct order for decisions to make from a leader, decisions will be slowed down due to research made to consider all interests. Implementing any decision that is decided would only make the organization spend more in revenue trying to acquaint and explore different perspectives.

In times of management crisis, leaders cannot wait for general opinions, which takes a lot of time to be made. Servant leaders might buckle under pressure to give out authoritative orders since they don't want the organization's policies and goals neglected. Now, this deviation from the norms of servant leader philosophy can lead to disastrous ends due to a lack of consultation on the best possible way out of the crisis.

It takes longer learning or retraining to be a servant leader

One of the most significant challenges that servant leadership has is that it is not easy to set it up when the organization was running another leadership style in the past. It is only when you start with the philosophy from the initial set-up of the organization that it is much easier to implement. It takes a lot of commitment and understanding from the leader and their team members for the implementation work for the growth of the organization.

Any attempt to effect a change from a former pattern of leadership to a servant leadership will have to come at the altar of some sacrifice. Employees and the leader of an organization would have to invest time, efforts, and money to learn, unlearn, and relearn every detail of servant leadership. There are no shortcuts to learning the tenets of the philosophy of servant leadership.

The role of the leader in the affairs of the organization is reduced

Being a servant leader means one has to always listen to what employees have to say that can benefit the organization. Since the leader only has to refuse requests which are not in the best interest of the organization, the leader is most like to stay put serving rather than leading. A leader should always assume the leadership position at all times to oversee the affairs of the organization. But he could be inhibited from doing this because of the long hours he puts into research and support ideas of team members.

Some positive thoughts might occur to the leader that he is heading the organization in the right direction. Yes! The interest in the growth of the company is being served already with great support from team members. But don't you think this would come with a heavy workload already. Trying to cover up one's essential duties as a leader as well as listen to team members for ideas could exhaust one from dispensing their duties.

Team members perceive the leader as vulnerable and try to take liberties

The honest motive of leading others by serving them first can be seen to be some sort of weakness. Team members could believe the leader is quite powerless because he tries to serve their interests more than himself first in decision making. Members could be led to believe such a scenario implies they are free from any sort of punishment for their actions. They could look to manipulate this perceived loophole to their selfish advantage.

Employees feel less motivated to perform their tasks

Servant leadership can make employees or team members feel less motivated and lackadaisical about completing their designated tasks. The very awareness of the natural tendency of the servant leader to step in to help them complete tasks they don't complete hinders their work rate. This is because they naturally feel relaxed about working since their leader always avails himself to help out. This could lead to employees not meeting the target and posting poor results for the organization.

It alienates from traditional leadership authority

With servant leadership comes the need for leaders to drop their authoritative roles in the organization. Servant leaders must be willing to shed away their regalia of absolute command and authority. This willingness truncates the role a traditional leader should play within a given workspace, making all the necessary decisions and communications to subordinates. It is left for the subordinates to fashion out a way to reach set targets by the leader who later claims recognition for every success made.

Servant leadership philosophy reduces the influence of the leader and their ego. The leader is no longer the center of decision making within the organization. Everyone has a role to play and is given credit for their contributions. This reduced role of the servant leader is what makes servant leadership all the more difficult to practice. It is rare to find anyone as a leader, business owner, or head of an organization who is ready to shed their authority for selfless leadership.

Managerial authority wanes

Placing the interests, ideas, and needs of one's team members first, of course, reduces the overall authority in the effective management of any establishment. When a leader portrays an extreme need to cater to all interests, from personal to professional goals, of their employees, they tend to see the leader as less of an authoritative figure.

The servant leadership problem here can come to the fore when the board of directors wants the leader or manager to push the team members to achieve some arduous tasks. The leaders will immediately have to assume a more authoritative or dominate role, which even he and their subordinates are not used to. There is a need to establish a strong difference between the boss and the employee so as not to jeopardize the effective running of an organization.

Servant leadership does not fit every business model

There are limitations to where a servant leadership can effectively help grow and develop business ideas and goals. Not every business model can benefit from the offerings of servant leadership's philosophy. Come to think of it, it takes a whole lot of time and commitment for everyone within an establishment to learn and practice to be servants while leading. On the record here is the immediate inability for members to maintain a stable working environment where it can be practiced. It is not to be expected that within the period of change that there will be much growth. Talk more of development within the organization. You can't expect leaders who worry more about employee interest to be able to make honest submissions, critiques, or decisions that prove decisive for better working performance.

Examples of how people have used servant leadership to make transformations

Putting everyone first has been employed in various aspects of human endeavors long before Greenleaf coined servant leadership. What this means is that its effect has long been seen in the lives of individuals, enterprises, and corporations.

From personal life to business, to public servants, to even biblical facts, we can tell what impacts have been made already using servant leadership. Hence, the need to share some essential examples of transformations that resulted from employing a servant leadership style. We would likely come to terms with the growth with significant development that accompanies the leadership style.

Examples of servant leadership in business

Servant leaders in business do not make noise of their rule of serving others first. This silence is why examples of servant leadership in business is not one of the easiest cases to come by. But with a proper glance and exploration of our present business environment, we can see various examples lying before us.

Let's take each of the business examples one after another and see if they indeed fulfill the conditions of the "best test."

FedEx's people-first philosophy and its success

The world largest express transport company, FedEx Express, established in 1971, gave insight into the success it has had using a people-first philosophy. Fred Smith, the company's founder and CEO, says that when people employed under you are prioritized first before any other thing, they will give their all to provide quality services[10]. From their enthusiastic participation in the company's business activities, profits will quickly skyrocket. This

---

10 https://newsroom.fedex.com/newsroom/fedex-attributes-success-people-first-philosophy/

priority of employees is precisely what he does for their business to remain as a driving force in the industry.

Servant leadership has led the company to develop a distinctive company culture that makes it unique in its business. It developed a policy placing how it prioritizes its sphere of activity- from People-Service-Profit (PSP). It is this philosophy that has helped it grow exponentially, develop, and remain one of the most competitive forces in its business.

FedEx PSP philosophy is founded upon the belief that establishing a positive work environment for its employees is a sure-fire way to encourage them to provide equal quality service to customers. It is no wonder it provides them with healthy programs and courses to develop their careers within FedEx. Programs such as the Tuition Assistance Program, Advance into Management (AiM), and Promotion from Within Policy are quality programs that have helped employees to grow their potentials. In turn, employees have repaid their employers with the delivery of quality customer services and relations.

Marriott's "taking care of its associates" philosophy

Another company whose success has been attributed to its foundation on a people-first philosophy is Marriott. Marriott was founded by J. Willard and his wife, Alice S. Marriott, in 1927 in collaboration with their business partner Hugh Colton[11]. The

---

11 https://www.marriott.com/about/culture-and-values/history.mi

company created five sets of beliefs or policies to help steer them towards growth and development by placing people first as its priority. Its views include putting people first, excellence, change, actions with integrity, and service to humanity. Marriott's first policy to take in every situation that presents itself is to place people first. Their policy states that taking care of one's business associates makes room for them to take care of the customers.

The happiness of associates or employees within one's business cycle is triggered when they are given much respect and priority. This has been the core philosophy and value of the Marriott company since it was founded. It is a part of the company's DNA that has allowed the company to consistently receive awards, growth, and development everywhere it is in the world today.

SAS encourages employees to be open about ideas

Analytics leader SAS has a long-standing policy of cultivating innovation habits in its employees. This employee innovative philosophy has led it to become one of the leading figures in the analytics industry for more than four decades. The company has created for itself a robust set of criteria to help boost its employees' abilities to think outside the box[12].

---

12 https://www.sas.com/en_us/whitepapers/mit-analytics-as-source-of-business-innovation-108763.html

We can at least tell that its ability to motivate its employees by putting their innovative capacities to work first has led it to creating cutting-edge innovations and visionary products. It has been able to set itself on a pace way beyond that of its competitors by the establishment of a culture that breeds contributions to developing newer approaches to solving problems.

It has come as no surprise that it was named by Fast Company magazine as the best workplace for innovators to work. Part of its special initiatives to drive its innovative growth is the establishment of the Big Ideas series. Employees are allowed to express their innovative creativity and leadership abilities before their fellow workers. Everyone is permitted to bring new ideas to the table, engage in experiments, fail, and continue with their research on innovations. This is one of the driving forces of its ability to keep the world awed by its innovations.

Examples of servant leadership in the Bible

Leadership from time immemorial is not a relatively new concept. It has always been the case from the beginning of time that humans have leaders or certain persons who guide them throughout their existence. Leaders in this context lead the people by assuming authority and power over them. The same can be said of scriptural truths and events, as seen in the Bible. However, the role of a leader leading their people was to change with the coming of Jesus Christ.

Jesus Christ turned the narrative of leadership around from a leader placing himself first, to a leader being a servant first. This kind of leadership expressed by Jesus was not the kind that was expected of him. People thought he was going to come from the family of royalty and assume authority, power, and lordship over Israel and its noisy neighbors.

The leadership to be followed, as expressed by Jesus in Matthew 20:25-28 (KJV), points to servant leadership. It says:

"But Jesus called them unto him, and said, Ye know that the princes of the Gentiles exercise dominion over them, and they that are great exercise authority upon them. But it shall not be so among you: but whosoever will be great among you, let him be your minister; And whosoever will be chief among you, let him be your servant: Even as the Son of man came not to be ministered unto, but to minister, and to give his life a ransom for many[13]."

The excerpt that is derived from the scriptural passage above is quite simple. Christ wants the aim of leadership to be service to man or women rather than the wielding of power and authority. Since all glory belongs to God, there is no need to make our names known for having great powers and authority. Whatever position or high place you are, you should see yourself as a servant of the people.

---

13 https://www.kingjamesbibleonline.org/Matthew-20-25/

Becoming a servant leader based on the biblical standards means one has to adhere to some critical qualities of a servant leader within the scriptures. Jesus Christ explicitly taught his disciples and those around him about the need for being servants first. This is the means in which the people can be led aright to God through their leaders (servant leaders).

Servant leaders should pursue integrity

Integrity has to do with the overall quality of being honest and capable of having strong moral or ethical principles. It can be argued that these are essential qualities of anyone aspiring to the position of a servant leader. This is primarily the foundational leadership quality upon which others are built. Jesus wants us to be as righteous and just as possible in every aspect of our endeavors. Our actions and inactions should speak for itself of our faith in God.

Proverbs 21:3 (KJV) expresses the need for integrity to assume any position of our desire. It says:

"To do justice and judgment
is more acceptable to the Lord than sacrifice[14]."

To assume the position of a servant leader, we should not place a priority on maneuvering, cheating those we want to serve. The calling to leadership here is way beyond placing a premium on corrupt means as a way of leading.

14 https://www.studylight.org/bible/kjv/proverbs/21-3.html

Now, the world of today tells us that to get to our places of desire, we should do our all to get there. But we all should seek the path the Bible and Jesus, in particular, says we should follow to lead. Philippians 4:8 (KJV) explicitly covers such vital lessons for all servant leaders. It states:

"Finally, brethren, whatsoever things are true, whatsoever things are honest, whatsoever things are just, whatsoever things are pure, whatsoever things are lovely, whatsoever things are of good report; if there be any virtue, and if there be any praise, think on these things[15]."

A leader filled with integrity portrays good character to be emulated by his or her followers. Remember, those who follow you tend to borrow from your way of life to live as their own. Let them see manifesting in you the need to be upright at all times.

Servant leaders should be humble

Humility has to do with a modest view of oneself. It is often characterized by a lack of arrogance and genuine gratitude for what one possesses. But how many persons can willingly and easily submit that they don't know it all?

Given our prideful human nature, humility is a complicated human trait to exhibit by anyone. So many are filled with feelings

---

15 https://www.biblegateway.com/passage/?search=Philippians%20 4:8&version=KJV

of self-knowledge, self-assurance, and self-confidence, resulting in them banishing thought of humble beginnings.

Jesus, in his teachings, asked that we give up all these character traits and embrace humility. To take up the calling of servant leaders that we are, we need to do away with anything that comes close to pride. Colossians 3:12 (KJV) explains this need for the acceptance of humility and calmness. That part of the book says:

> *"Put on therefore, as the elect of God, holy and beloved, bowels of mercies, kindness, humbleness of mind, meekness, longsuffering[16]."*

In being true servant leaders from the Christian example here, those who are called to leadership positions should always be ready to learn from those who follow. No one knows it all. Leaders should be prepared to help and learn from their followers whenever or wherever they can. Those moments to share knowledge and experience could be decisive in your leading or misleading others. Your level of wisdom, knowledge, and experience should be built around the ability to take up useful suggestions and advice from others.

Make decisions when given the task to do so. Allow them to know you cherish their useful suggestions from time to time. There are times when they have brighter ideas than you might.

---

[16] https://biblehub.com/colossians/3-12.htm

This implies that a servant leader should always have a listening hear to be able to receive some insightful ideas from his followers.

The flexibility of a servant leader is held in high regard

It is not every day that one is called to a leadership position to be a servant to the people. Servant leaders, when given the task to lead, should embrace the responsibility of stepping into leadership positions. They should be ready to accept the gauntlet of leadership and should do a great job of being flexible.

When a leader assumes a leadership position, it is expected that the situation will be unfamiliar and chaotic. Life throws different challenges and situations that are not expected often. It is only those who can maneuver (be flexible) their way around situations that come out on top.

The place of God, who is seen as the author and finisher of the Christian faith, is recognized. Since he is there to guide you through every process of the way, cease from looking towards events that bring more confusion, anger, and anxiety to the calling of a leader. This is the only way change, growth, and development can be affected on the lives of the people.

Philippians 4:12-13 aptly covers the need to look towards God when leading the people. There is and should be no concern about things that are meant to be a part of one's endeavor in the world in which we live. Scripture says:

"I know both how to be abased, and I know how to be abound: everywhere and in all things I am instructed both to be full and to be hungry, both to abound and to suffer need. I can do all things through Christ which strengtheneth me[17]."

The place of resilience in service leadership

Resilience has to do with the ability or capacity to spring back quickly from problems and difficulties. Now, this ability or function is given by God to man (service leaders), so they don't fall away from the path of growing in faith and seeking his face. They are made all the stronger for placing their trust in the leadership of God to lead their lives.

Resiliency within the context of biblical standards has to do with the spiritual capacity to endure challenging situations. A perfect example of this can be found in Hebrews 12:1-2 (KJV). It is said that man should put away every hindrance to reaching the goals of the kingdom of God by enduring to the end. It says:

"Wherefore seeing we also are compassed about with so great a cloud of witnesses, let us lay aside every weight and the sin which doth so easily beset us, and let us run with patience the race that is set before us. Looking unto Jesus the author and finisher of our faith; who for the joy that was set before him endured the cross, despising the shame, and is set down at the right hand of the throne of God[18]."

Service leaders should be able to recognize that all challenges, difficulties, and problems are a part of livelihood. But they

---

17 https://biblehub.com/kjv/philippians/4-12.htm

18 https://www.kingjamesbibleonline.org/Hebrews-12-1/

should be quick to note that at all times they continue the race of leading, their God is in total control. It is only the strength of God as seen from his shield, promises, and protection over his people; that is all that is needed.

Service leaders should not be afraid of failing in their tasks. What they should caution themselves against is not trying to stand up to their feet again. This is one of the unique qualities that is needed to be exhibited from such a leader.

The place of stewardship

Stewardship is a critical quality of a servant leader that differentiates him from power-drunken leaders. Stewardship as defined by Merriam-Webster's dictionary is "conducting, supervising, or managing of something. Especially the careful and responsible management of something entrusted to one's care[19]." This implies that servant leaders should tread with great care when leading those who are placed under their supervision.

The Bible captures the role of a steward steering God's people towards greater heights in 1 Peter 4:10 (KJV). That part of the book says:

> "As every man hath received the gift, even so minister the same one to another, as good stewards of the manifold grace of God[20]."

---

[19] https://www.merriam-webster.com/dictionary/stewardship
[20] https://biblehub.com/1_peter/4-10.htm

Everyone is born with at least a talent or two to use to project the grace and glory of God. With the various spiritual gifts given to every human, there is a need for them to be in charge of a leader (steward). This is where the servant leader comes in to play a significant role in the lives of God's people.

A steward steers God's people who have been placed under his care towards the direction of God's kingdom. He sees the gifts of God manifesting in everyone and helps them see value in themselves and the sight of God. He takes up the task of harnessing, instructing, and encouraging everyone to serve the purpose of God.

Now, in corporate affairs and leadership, a servant leader should look to make everyone works in tandem for the growth of the organization. Serving the people by providing them with encouragement, motivation, help, and finally letting them see you value them moves them. They are spurred by those acts you showed them to deliver the goals the organization sets out to achieve.

Steward leaders should show empathy

Empathy has to do with the ability to be able to understand other people's points of view or the consequences of such views other than your own. Possessing this quality or ability is what enables us to see the pains, anxiety, shame, fears, sadness, joy, excitement, and amusement of others and share a part of it with them. Sharing empathy with others means to see what they go through and help them feel a sense of belonging, whether it is a positive or negative occurrence.

A servant leader should possess this essential leadership quality of empathy. There is a need always to understand what those you lead are going through. Of course, this is what enables a leader to know how to help or assuage any situation his or her people go through. Putting your people to work on targets set out by an organization is excellent. But stretching your employees without identifying them as humans to be loved can be detrimental. Understand what they go through, and it would be easier for them to work on set-out goals.

Understanding those around you and empathizing with them makes us more like Jesus. Jesus felt compassion for many after he understood their plights. He then moved to make them feel much better than they felt before he met them. This is what a servant leader should do when called to a leadership position.

Romans 12:15 (KJV) is the scripture to be dwelled upon by those who assume leadership positions. Jesus directed those who follow him and those who lead to take the same stance of empathy each time they come across people. It says:

"Rejoice with them that do rejoice, and weep with them that weep[21]."

---

21 https://www.biblehub.com/kjv/romans/12-15.htm

Examples of servant leadership in public servants

The practice of servant leadership should be encouraged in various industries, careers, and public service. This leadership quality servant leader brings to the table is sure to bring about positive results, growth, and development. Despite this need, servant leadership is welcome and utilized in some spheres for the management and organization of corporations than others.

You must have asked yourself an important question on servant leadership already. Why does servant leadership need to vary across industries and corporations? Reasons why servant leadership utility varies from corporation or industries depends on their perceived need for the principle. Let's consider some of the places where the need for servant leadership is needed for public service.

Education

One vital industry where servant leadership can thrive and is much needed is that of education. Servant leadership is very crucial to the success of schools' educational climate. The positivity that is brought to fore when everyone tends to serve within the education industry ensures that students' needs are met.

Let's consider, for instance, that school A and school B are two schools operating under two distinct leadership cultures: servant leader and traditional authoritative culture, respectively.

School A has imbibed servant leadership that is portrayed by the principal to the teachers themselves. Everyone within the system strives to work collectively by helping each other achieve tasks and goals set up for the school. This kind of relationship will surely be caught on by the students too, who could prove to be present and future servant leaders.

On the other hand, school B is led by your everyday traditional leadership culture. The principal relays rules, obligations, and commitments down to the teachers with authority. Yes! There is no gain saying that these obligations would be met occasionally by the teachers. But in the long run, teachers will feel tired and less motivated to bring about better results. They may tend to expose students to their loss of motivation, allowing students to bear the brunt of their displeasure.

Service leadership as seen in school A allows the focus on students' development to spark more commitment than has been observed. Now, if you as an administrator intend to search for teachers, you would want those who can have an impact on students like teachers who wish to serve rather than show off their lead to students.

Government

Service leadership is not quite rampant within government circles. But they do make sure to demand those who are servant leaders to help reach their constituents better. Some roles like career public service employees, military and many more help the government to function better.

So much sacrifice is needed from public personnel recruited to work for government parastatals. This is so because the government is a direct representation of the people. To represent the people properly, there is a need to serve them as a means of leadership. Hence, public servants who are servant leaders are highly sought after to be recruited by the government.

Healthcare

The role the health sector has to play in the proper functioning of the society is so significant. Look at the recent pandemic of the coronavirus. If it wasn't for the unselfless work, our world would be different today. The health sector is such that it is defined by the standards, values, and institutions that aid the production and distribution of goods and services meant to secure the health status of individuals.

From here, we can see that the healthcare sector aims to take care of the sick, research for newer ways of protecting the health of people and prevent and control available diseases. What role does a servant leader play in the health sector?

To answer, one needs to consider the critical instrument the health sector plays in the furtherance of human existence. Miserable servitude or leadership from healthcare workers could lead to the easy termination of human life, increase the mortality rate (that is, reduced number of births and an increase in the number of deaths), and poor access to quality healthcare, and so on.

The health sector is only made better when healthcare workers feel that moral obligation and dedication to the people. This is the tenet or underlying principle that guides the system. Can you see what servant leadership does to the health system? The direct contact and interaction health workers have with patients on a daily basis are numerous. To retain the trust people have in them, they have to possess that serving attitude at all times.

Non-profit (NPO)

Non-profit organizations, voluntary services, and many more are always in search of those who want to serve great causes. Why? Because only those who can be committed and dedicated at all times to selfless service are needed.

Most non-profit organizations are run at low cost, and, generally, there is not a lot to use to pay staff members. Hence, the need for those who are more concerned about their servitude to the people rather than for the motive of making extravagant amounts of money.

Call to ministry or religious leadership

Many religions in the world emphasize the need for servitude towards everyone. Be it those who are outside of one's religious beliefs, most religions say we should show all human love, compassion, and care at all times.

The nature of religion itself suggests the humility and servitude of those who work within religious circles. There are many great examples of religions that emphasize total dedication to their religion, its members and even those who don't practice the religion.

Chapter Two
POSITIONAL SERVANT

A positional servant exhibits the character traits of a leader who operates from a traditional leadership position. In the traditional leadership setting, when a person assumes the status of a leader, he is immediately given all or most of the power to run an organization. The power of such a leader comes from the rights and privileges of the position of office they occupy. They wields much control over those he or she leads and can hardly be questioned for his or her decisions on essential matters.

The leadership path taken by a positional leader is in contrast with a servant leader upon the assumption of office. The positional servant called to serve as a leader commands respect from their peers and followers based on the title of their office. Much attention is not given to the implications of his or her authoritative leadership and what it does to the organization in which he is called to lead.

This positional leadership trait is nothing other than authoritarian in nature. What this leadership's (positional servant) characteristics imply is that the only influence the leader has on members of staff is linked to the power of his or her office to coerce them to action. This shows how great the misunderstanding leaders who practice such styles have of how great leaders command commitment and loyalty from followers.

The concern of the boss (positional servant) is often on the extent to which they can use their power to dictate proceedings in the organization. This is to say that the processes or tempo of how the organization and management of the enterprise works solely relies on them. No interest whatsoever is given by the leader to the impact of their leadership on the performance of staff, their welfare, general behavior, and attitude to the goals set out by the organization.

Positional leaders are respected based on the authority of their office, rather than on natural clout. Their leadership does not earn any iota of trust or respect from workers. Most times they resort to tyranny, blackmail, and threatening of staff with getting sacked if they don't get the job done. This does not create a healthy environment for workers to be able to compete amongst themselves to grow and develop the organization.

In the present time, the servant leadership style has started to take great shape- a leader puts their followers ahead of every other thing. Ken Blanchard says, "In the past, a leader was a boss.

Today's leaders must be partners with their people...they no longer can lead solely based on positional power[22]."

Implications of adopting positional leadership

Positional leadership, just like every other leadership style, has some general implications. It's not all negative implications for positional leadership, so we should not criticize it generally. There are also some positive insights to receive from the application of position in leadership.

Positive implications of positional leadership

Some positive high points of positional leadership might make you want to consider being a servant leader. Although this is a top position to start, I don't think it is one leadership position where you should aim to remain.

Positional leadership helps identify the potentials of being a leader

The appointment of persons to the position of leadership is usually based on the identification of leadership potentials. This category of leaders is appointed by those in authority (managers, the board of directors) to help manage a position. Most times, the growth in the organization's operations reflects on the need for more staff strength and an increase in departments. By implication, there will always arise the need to appoint leaders to oversee the new spaces.

22 https://www.brainyquote.com/quotes/ken_blanchard_173324

Appointment to the position of leadership is based solely on the potentials identified and not on one's qualifications, senior rank, or politics. This act indeed shows the confidence those in authority have in the potentials of the newly appointed leader. That's a pass mark or a vote of confidence in their abilities and contributions towards taking the organization to greater heights.

At this stage of leadership, it calls for celebration because this is a start towards learning the ropes of leadership. It is at this point you begin to have an idea of what leadership entails-making decisions, carrying others, hitting desired targets, etc. But this should not be the leading point you intend to stay at for too long

Recognition of authority

When a person is appointed to the position of leadership, it is expected that they have been given some level of authority, power, or free reign. This authority bestowed on them is not a license to take laws into one's own hands. Instead, it is for a leader to recognize their role as the person who oversees the affairs of the organization or workplace. An excerpt taken from the *Infantryman's Journal* goes thus: "No man is a leader until his appointment is ratified in the minds and the hearts of men[23]."

Usually, the power invested in the newly appointed leader is just a bit of the power that resides with the management or

---

23 https://thearmyleader.co.uk/leadership-quotes/

board of directors. It is left for the positional leader to prove their mettle and worth with the little authority he or she is given.

Position of leadership is an invitation to grow as a leader

Great leaders don't get to be celebrated in a day or a matter of weeks or months. They took a long time to grow by learning the ropes of leadership each day. It is expected that once a leader takes off on the path of growth, they should transcend positional leadership.

New leaders should dedicate their time to radical development each day. It is only by making improvements on one's qualities and leadership capabilities that one can get more success for the people and organization. Vince Lombardi says "leaders are made; they are not born[24]." They are made by hard effort, which is the price which all of us must pay to achieve any worthwhile goal. Therefore, it is our responsibility to learn and grow more as leaders so we can guide our steps and that of others aright.

Positional leadership allows potential leaders to define and shape their leadership

Being appointed to the role of a positional leader allows potential leaders to determine what kind of leader they want to be. This is a time to think and reflect on what type of leadership

---

24 https://greatist.com/fitness/quote-football-vince-lombardi-091612#1

characteristics you wish to exhibit. It is in your powers alone to decide what kind of a leader you want to make your followers see you as. Do you want them to see you as autocratic, tyrannical, or you want to be known as a loving and caring leader? Do you want to be recognized as a leader with vision, foresight, and direction or a leader who knows absolutely nothing and is blown away by the tide? This and many more reasonable questions should be answered to develop a leadership style that suits you.

Whatever decision you make, it should be done with plans for consistency. Consistency allows your employees to know what principles you stand for on a personal level and at the workplace. It's left to you to make a decision that could either make or mar your journey towards becoming a great leader.

Negative implications of positional leadership

Positional leadership has quite a large number of negative implications in contrast to its positive consequences. I will take you through some of the impacts of practicing or remaining a positional leader.

Positional leadership often misleads

Being called to occupy a position of authority or leadership as a potential leader is excellent. However, the level of performance of the leader seems to be quite static. There is nothing that indicates that one is a leader beyond the position that one occupies. The belief that those who are called to positions of power would get the job done is baseless.

Positional leadership is reliant on politics

The focus of positional leadership is on the powers that reside in the office of appointment. Rather than emphasize influencing or making others contribute their quota to the development of an organization, positional leadership relies on coercion, force, and authority to get work done.

Leaders who place value on coercion, just like positional leaders, do create some sort of political atmosphere within the organization. It makes other group leaders try to jostle to control the more substantial space within the organization. The focus then shifts from working on completing organization goals to who has more control of positional power over the people and departments. This consequentially creates an unhealthy work environment filled with rivalry, constant bickering, and individualism.

Rights is placed over and above responsibilities by positional leaders

Robert Greenleaf says, "Ego can't sleep. It micro-manages. It disempowers. It reduces our capability. It excels in control[25]." Positional leaders, most times, rely on the powers and rights given to them by the authorities or management. They don't

---

25 https://www.azquotes.com/quote/1384630

think towards shared responsibility or teamwork, which is deserving of their workplace. Placing rights above responsibility does more harm than good to the workplace because it creates a broad distinction between the leader and the people. The people are made to serve the leader's interests alone rather than the leader serving those he leads.

The great poet, T. A. Elliot, says, "Half of the harm that is done in this world is due to people who want to feel important[26]." Great leaders don't always want to emphasize their position among the people. Yes! It is a given that a leader is the one with the powers, but the use of these powers should be used to the benefits of the people rather than for personal gratification. The position of power should not be used to make any one individual more important than the people as a whole. This is why people feel a sense of belonging when they are given a part or responsibility in making changes for the society or organization.

Reliance on position to lead devalues the people

What means do you use to devalue those you lead than to engage in positional leadership? Positional leaders place much more premium on their leadership than on the actual people they lead. They don't tend to think highly of those who they work alongside. The office they occupy is something closer to

---

26 https://www.goodreads.com/quotes/101806-half-the-harm-that-is-done-in-this-world-is

being a "god," what with the way they exhale the position above all things.

The focus of leadership is meant to serve and bring people from different backgrounds together as one. But the positional leader does not realize this point, as he thinks their position is the real deal. They feels the only stumbling block to their achievement of set-out goals are the employees. This disposition does not promote good rapport and relations between the people and the organization they serve. It drops the rate of team solidarity and morale.

There is loneliness in positional leadership

One feature common to positional leaders is that they are rather lonely most of the time. These leaders have set for themselves a space separate from the people they are called to lead. They set this space apart with the belief that they occupy a position more prominent than others, and as such, others should not encroach.

Positional leadership at its height is a misunderstanding of the basic reasons for establishing leadership. Leadership is about working alongside with the people you lead, helping them to reach both individual and collective goals. You can't boldly declare to have attained organizational goals without the people being a part of it.

Positional leaders get branded and stuck

Leading from a positional leadership perspective for too long creates negative impressions on the people. Leaders like this always fail in their quest to impress or influence the decisions of people. People brand them as positional leaders who go on to become stuck in the same position. They are no longer trusted to handle higher positions of power because of their lack of influence on the lives of the people.

Positional leaders are to realize that it is not the position they occupy that makes them leaders. Instead, it should be the leader in him that defines the position of leadership. This is a call to positional leaders to reverse their stance on prioritizing position above the people. The fourth chapter of this book is dedicated to helping you move away from placing priority on position to what is more important, which is the people.

Positional leadership encourages below-par performance from the people

Positional leadership reduces the eagerness and team spirit of workers to work towards achieving targets. Leaders rely on getting things done through the use of their powers without even doing much work. People also adopt this stance of doing little at work based on the bad example shown by the positional leader. This leads to reduced productivity from every corner.

Innovative and ambitious people are more likely to burn out the fire with which they started with while working for an organization. People's productivity tends to be reduced when they are less motivated by their leaders or the environment. It is only the motivated person who is always ready to go the extra mile even after completion of the work for the day without being told to do so. Workers here just work to pass away time.

John Maxwell describes the people under the positional leadership condition as "clock-watchers[27]." These workers don't give their 100% at work. They do what is needed to be done and immediately start looking forward to closing hours. They are just absent-minded people whose physical bodies are present in the workplace. It tells a lot of the kind of leadership used in the workplace if workers are always absent-minded.

For positional leaders, turnover is high

The effect of relying too much on position for leadership is that it yields high turnover, says John Maxwell. People tend to quit their workplaces most of the time because of a bad boss who relies too much on the power that resides in their office to get them to work. It does not necessarily have to do with the company rules and regulations in the first place.

---

27 https://neoralston.wordpress.com/2013/12/04/upsides-and-downsides-of-positional-leadership/

Positional leaders, most times, bend the rules and regulations of an organization to suit their desires. This leads to people quitting because of their torture and power drunkenness, and as such, experts might be forced to leave. Now, those experts who leave are often hard to replace, given that there are not many knowledgeable people in various fields.

Chapter Three
TIMES ARE CHANGING IN TERMS OF LEADERSHIP QUALITY AND STANDARD

The world, as we know it today, is not the same way it used to be in the past. Every second(s), minute(s), hour(s), day(s), week(s), month(s) and year(s), there seem to be one or two changes effected in the universe. Humans, as they are, are not immune to these changes. This is proof of the nature of the universe and the constant urge of man to adapt to its changes by themselves changing their ways.

Humans have gone through different historical developments over time, which is attributed to natural manifestations. ese natural manifestations have resulted in changes that are evident in our lives today. From human development in technological innovations to political structuring, from agricultural innovations to healthcare, etc, there has been a lot of changes. is quickly brings to mind Heraclitus's (the ancient philosopher) dictum, where he likened life to a river in constant ux.

Changes in leadership style

Leadership has also endured lots of changes in the present, as it is no longer the way it used to be in the past. In the past, leadership was awash with authoritative, tyrannical, and positional campaigns whenever a leader came to power. It was characterized by the ability to rely on physical, military, or mental superiority or force to coerce others into submission to one's authority.

Now the world is at a stage where leadership is defined by a leader's evident ability and foresight to carry their followers along by showing care and servitude towards them. This does not only apply to the functioning of government institutions, but also the organization and management of enterprises, corporations, personal human relationships, etc. This prompts Theodore Roosevelt's insightful statement to come to the fore: "Nobody cares how much you know, until they know how much you care[28]."

A person is more reckoned now for their ability to carry those around him along. It is not just about democracy, which has swept up most parts of the world in terms of leadership. It is about being able to command enough respect from people to commit and influence them to carry out simple and challenging tasks. Be you a government executive, a leader in the church, a father, a director, or a manager, your sphere of influence is only

---

28 https://www.brainyquote.com/quotes/theodore_roosevelt_140484

recognized when you are believed to care about what your people desire sincerely. This is merely putting them first in everything you do rather than the aggrandizement of your authority over them.

Having covered the change in leadership style, I would like to go through the different levels of developing leadership skills. The different levels of the development of leadership skills will take us closer to placing our followers first. It gives an insight into the present leadership style that has taken over from positional leadership.

The different stages of developing leadership skills

Developing leadership qualities and traits comes with lots of hard work and dedication. Leadership skills, when properly understood, can help increase one's ability to influence others. These qualities can help build trust, connection, and maintain cordial relationships among co-workers if put to proper use.

Although many theories abound on ways to develop one's leadership qualities, I am very much enamored with John Maxwell's leadership stages. Its levels project the growth of leadership from a positional servant's struggles with leadership to the high points of servant leadership.

Maxwell provides five levels of leadership, which would be succinctly discussed to aid our general understanding steps towards becoming a servant leader[29]. We would see what personal interaction and care of others around us can support great achievements while in leadership positions.

The stage of position

The position leadership stage is the foundational level of any leadership quality or skill. Any leader at this level assumes power or authority based on some circumstances that cannot be described as merit. People are not appointed at this point based on their past or present abilities to lead others effectively. Instead, leaders may be appointed because of their closeness to power (heirs to thrones, kingdoms, etc.) or the mere fact that there is a need to fill a position based on time spent working within the confines of power or an establishment. Anyone can be called to fill in an empty leadership space because of the increase in the number of departments within an organization.

The implication of a positional leader's ascension to power is not based on their quality of leadership experience. Leaders within this stage are naïve about the knowledge of showing care, understanding, and the ability to influence those they lead to show commitment or support towards their leadership. Since they don't realize or know how to influence others, they result to the use of their office to lead and command others to act. They will always find a way of resorting to company policies, rules, and regulations to control everyone to work.

[29] https://graduateway.com/5-levels-of-leadership-by-john-maxwell/

At this stage of leadership, there is no shared personal relationship between the boss and theirs team. What they share is the workspace and the need to work towards meeting an organization's targets. This working relationship means that workers don't show trust and commitment towards the leader. They only respect them because of the office or position they occupy.

Only smart leaders can transcend the position stage of leadership. They can realize that placing themselves first before their employees do more harm than good to their image and that of the growth of the organization.

The stage of permission

The permission stage of leadership skill or quality defines that point where a leader has built around themselves personal and close relationship with their employees. At this stage, there is something somewhat of a passive vote of confidence/permission given to the boss leadership. The team working around them are in no doubt that their leader is someone who can be trusted with taking essential and decisive decisions.

Why the sudden change in the acknowledgement of the boss leadership at this stage? Here, the leader has gone beyond the point of using their position to achieve results. They realize soon enough that making little sacrifices to know the workers is a better "position" to take. The leader then quickly takes the needs of the workers seriously, by bridging the gap that once existed in their relationship at the position stage.

Employees become easily motivated, not just from themselves alone, but also by the belief their leader has in them. They become more relaxed in the new working atmosphere and easily develop team spirit and partnership. It is this new relationship that enables workers to put more vigor and hard work towards repaying the trust, belief, and confidence the leader has in them. But it does not necessarily follow that the results achieved at this stage would turn out to be positive.

The stage of production

The production stage has to do with the results of a leader's leadership that could be measured. Here, we are looking at what role and impacts the leader have played in the development of the organization. The concern is from their personal and work relationship with workers to their contribution to the entire growth of the organization and so on.

The fact remains that a leader will attain more growth and development for their organization by building excellent relationships with those under them. Just like the famous saying, "A tree does not make a forest," a leader cannot expect to deliver the goals all by himself. Workers are also essential towards getting targeted results. This is only made possible by the kind of relationship the boss has with the workers.

Enforcing workers to work alone without any slight thoughts of their plights is counterproductive. People tend to quickly burn out of energy and fire when little interest is given thought about them. Leaders at this stage of leadership instead enforce some level of cooperation, teamwork, and team spirit by building a strong personal relationship with workers. They go out of their way to improve the skills of the workers, thereby leading to higher productivity. Workers, in turn, deliver outstanding and quality jobs to repay their leaders for the understanding and confidence reposed in them.

The strong personal relationship the leader sets leads to exponential growth and development. The leader who commands trust and commitment from employees sets out tasks and goals that everyone follows, including themselves. However, the growth and development brought about by the relationship between the leader and their employees is short-lived. The whole system collapses once the leader leaves the leadership position for a higher place or another job. This goes to show that team is reliant on the guidance of the leader for their every move.

The stage of people development

The people development stage is way higher than the first three stages in terms of the development and encouragement of employees. This fourth stage of leadership is where the leader helps to coach and empower employees with the requisite skills to develop their careers. These skills help them to excel in a personal level and for the growth of the organization.

Priority at this stage of leadership is given to the development of employees far above the personal interest of the leader. The employees are not only trained to be better at what they do, they are also groomed to become future leaders whether it's within the organization or outside it. So, it's important to groom better employees than to place priority on getting results or goals met. It is no wonder a leader at this stage spends most of their time teaching others rather than on their input or productivity.

It is at this fourth stage of leadership that the foundation for servant leaders to flourish is laid; that is, leaders who serve the interest of others are raised and put to work throughout the organization. An organization that employs these tactics of the fourth stage of leadership is sure to have much more success growing and developing.

The pinnacle stage

The pinnacle stage is the final level of leadership. It is at this stage that the servant leader is fully born and given the power to reign. Their peers highly respect the leader here for their dedication, exemplary lifestyle, excellent communication, integrity, and so on. A leader within this stage remains on the minds of their employees even after the close of work each day or when they bow out of the organization.

I will like to call leaders at this last stage "servant leaders," under whose leadership organizations move forward. It is under their watch that an enabling environment for learning, coupled with chances of higher productivity, reaches the roofs. The leaders here make it a priority that they provide listening ears to their employees, allow employees a say in some decision making, and so on.

To fully understand how to become servant leaders, which is the purpose of the last chapter, we need to realize what makes servant leadership different from the "traditional leadership" style. There is a need to comprehend the gains that could be gained from dropping traditional leadership and sticking to servant leadership. To do this, we need first to take a cursory look at the concept of traditional leadership.

What is traditional leadership

Traditional leadership refers to the leadership style of given powers to leaders based on past traditions, rules, and origins. Power is handed over because of the relationship that is shared with the new leader and the past. Kings, queens, families, and friends of dictators, and some leaders in the present business world are excellent examples of traditional leadership.

Several years ago, leadership was always about those who share some closeness to the former leader or ruler. Power resided in the traditions and origins of the kingdom, organization, and enterprise. Traditional leadership comes in the form of positional leadership in organizations of today. The leaders have no power whatsoever apart from that of the office they occupy.

Leaders who ascend to power via traditional means or positional leadership are characterized by their reliance on their ability to maximize the powers and authority of their position. They make decisions solely on the powers that reside in their office(s), rendering workers loyal to the office. Workers maintain loyalty to the office occupied to get work done, rather than on the influence of the personality of the leader.

Traditional leadership differs from servant leaders in so many ways. It's not just based on the different methods of ascension to the position of authority alone, but also to the ideologies and motives of leadership in the two cases. It will do well to clarify their differences so we can see why it's best to hang on to servant leadership. This will prepare us for the knowledge of how to become servant leaders in the next chapter.

Differences between traditional leadership and servant leadership

Several differences exist between traditional and servant leadership. From the basic foundation of leadership to their ideologies, we will see that their differences abound.

Ascension to a leadership position

A traditional leader comes to the position of power or authority based solely on their proximity to the traditions and origins of society or organization. It is challenging to see leaders under this category who don't have any contact whatsoever with the throne. Sometimes leaders here come to the position of power by seizing leader forcefully from an incumbent leader (through coups, etc.).

On the other hand, a servant leader comes to power based on their cordial relationship with others who "root" for their leadership. Not all leaders who are servant leaders are born that way. Some are self-taught leaders who establish a cordial relationship with the people. Hence, the people offer support and a vote of confidence for their leadership.

The place of the followers in decisions made

Traditional leaders who lack the backing or trust of the general public don't have legitimate influence over the people to make commitments. Most times, they are autocratic, despotic, and tyrannical, dealing with their subjects. They resort to the powers that reside in their leadership office or position to command people to act. Any attempt to go contrary or murmur against leaders like this could lead to punishments depending on the discretion of the leader. Hence, the leader priorities himself above those he rules over. Modern-day positional leaders fall under this category of traditional leaders.

The servant-leader is not power-driven like the traditional ruler, because he sees himself as a servant to the people first before any other thing. He places priority over the needs of those who have been placed under their leadership, serving their needs. The servant-leader consciously has feelings within himself of the need to help the people. It is not the case that someone just placed it in their mind that he would inherit leadership later on. This conscious thought is what drives them to the position of power to actualize the will of the people. Democratic leaders in government and organizations fall under this category.

Now, since the leader places a priority on serving people first, it is important to note that decisions made would be people-oriented. Both the leader and the people share powers when it comes to making decisions that are meant for all. They are open to the brilliant opinions of followers who proffer solutions to problems at every stage of the way. What this implies is that the leader makes sure that whatever decision that is made must be to serve the people better.

The care and guidance provided for followers

Although the traditional leader enhances some form of encouragement to the people to be productive at their jobs, they do it intending to improve their organization or their society.

They do not care about the need to enhance the knowledge and skills of their followers intrinsically. They are more concerned about what reputation or name they can make for themselves as the one who effects positive change to the organization.

The servant leader, on the other hand, takes a different path. Their utmost concern is that the needs of the people are met. To make this happen, they offer them constant motivation, support, and guidance in the right direction. Servant leaders take up the responsibility of seeing that their followers become better persons in their careers or chosen field, personal development, etc. To this end, they take up the challenge of teaching them to improve themselves and become more productive.

Consequences of traditional leadership and servant leadership on employee productivity

There is no gainsaying that productivity can be enhanced when a traditional leader emerges as a leader to specific persons. But we cannot underestimate the fact that the autocratic nature of a leader could be a killjoy on the people's drive towards completion of set-out tasks. In contrast, the servant leader brings the people together to work as one. The people cultivate team spirit as they work on getting tasks done. This cordial relationship the workers share amongst themselves, between them and the leader, could lead to exponential growth and development.

High points gotten from the differences between traditional leadership and servant leadership

From the look of things, it is crystal clear that traditional leadership fails to establish cordial working relations between a leader and their employees. Workers only work for the leader because of the fear of their wrath (the fear of being fired or resignation to fate, etc.). They don't feel a sense of completeness working under the traditional leader, thereby creating an unhealthy working atmosphere. We cannot help but look towards servant leadership as the better of the two leadership styles. The concreteness of the established relationship with all team members is enough to set the pace for an organization's growth.

Chapter Four
BECOMING A SERVANT LEADER

Becoming a great leader means one has to be a great follower indeed first, that is, one has to serve the people first. The most result-driven-oriented leaders can achieve better results only if they dedicate themselves more towards followership than leadership first. This is, as Mahatma Gandhi says, "The best way to find yourself is to lose yourself in the service of others[30]." Leaders who tend to place the needs of their workers above the results they want from them consequently achieve better results than those who do otherwise.

There is no gain saying the importance of becoming a servant leader who the best interest of their employees at heart. Placing the benefit of your employees at heart does not imply that one should give one's workers the liberties to misbehave. There should be rules and regulations set up about what is expected from employees at every given time. But this does not derail the

---

30 https://www.brainyquote.com/quotes/mahatma_gandhi_150725

leader from showing them care and a sense of belonging at all times.

With all the above said, I would like to share the reasons why you should choose to become a servant leader in case you decide to lead. There are many such reasons, but I will share a few of them here. These reasons should serve as a motivation for you to learn to become a servant leader.

Servant leadership builds strong culture(s)

The establishment of servant leadership within an organization helps build a unique working culture. Servant leadership creates an organization's culture on the foundation of team spirit, togetherness, service to one another, and the community far above gains. This, in turn, does wonder to the mentality, growth, and development of workers and the organization. It rubs off on the minds of our followers the knowledge that they work within an exclusive establishment that cherishes everyone for their contributions. People hardly want to walk away from where they get lots of joy and happiness.

Servant leadership increases the rate of innovation

More often than not, innovative ideas are birthed in conducive environments where there are risks and liberties. Servant leadership allows the creation of this type of environment for the growth and development of its workers. The underlying principle of servant leadership is to create a space where people are encouraged to dispute the present state of things, air their views to things, and to take risks if need be. This fosters the ability for innovations to be rapidly made since everyone aspires to proffer newer ways of doing things.

Servant leadership gives a new sense of purpose

Servant leadership gives leaders a different purpose with which to achieve. This purpose is quite different from the mere need to work as a leader or to achieve set-out goals for one's organizations. It has to do with working towards creating a team that can work in tandem and harmony toward the same purpose. It is undoubtedly exciting when you think of the prospect of being the leader of a group who serves, dotes, and cares for themselves and others around them. There is nothing more eventful than your followers or employees aspiring to exhibit the same qualities they see in you. This is the kind of purpose you should want to possess as a leader.

Servant leadership helps improve customer service

The energy you exude to those you lead will reflect in the way they treat others, especially your customers. The singular act of care, empathy, and humility a servant leader shows to their employees is an imprint on their minds. They, in turn, go on to replicate this same attitude towards customers, giving them valuable and quality service that none can rival. This, in turn, drives much more results than even envisaged by the management in the first place.

Servant leadership achieves its success in a different way

The servant leadership philosophy discourages emphasizing profits or personal self. Instead, it encourages leaders to be more concerned about making people feel their service, love, and care. This essential "service" in the long run drives a higher return of success and profitability to the organization.

The shift of one's business from profits alone creates a new criterion for determining success. Success here would be determined by how much people enjoy working, how much they grow on a personal and professional level, and how much they are being groomed towards becoming servant leaders themselves. This is an undaunting challenge every servant leader takes on.

An understanding of these reasons highlighted above should be considered in line with what achievements you want to accomplish as a leader. Taking the right decision to become a servant leader has many prospects of catapulting you beyond what you think. With this said, I would like to take you through on some steps towards becoming the servant leader you want to be. There are 12 attributes of servant leaders that have adequately passed scrutiny. These 12 attributes should be practiced, one for each month, as building blocks towards becoming a servant leader.

12 easy steps on how to become a servant leader

Becoming a servant leader takes more than the mere desire to become one. There is that part of the conscious activity of practicing towards becoming a committed and dedicated servant leader. Servant leadership possesses several attributes that distinguish a servant leader from a traditional leader. These 12 attributes are to be practiced to help fine tune you towards becoming the best servant leader you can be.

The 12 attributes to learn are as follows;

Empathy

Empathy is one of the attributes that best describes a servant leader. The Merriam-Webster dictionary defines empathy as "the imaginative projection of a subjective state into an object so that the object appears to be infused with it[31]." What this implies is that a servant leader possesses the capability to quickly look at their team and recognize their emotional states and feelings. They make sure to place themselves in their shoes to determine what point of view they presently have before making any decision.

The ability of a leader to understand their team members' plight and feelings allows the leader to show them care and help them whenever the need arises. If you don't have an understanding of their points of view, you will hardly be able to

[31] https://www.merriam-webster.com/dictionary/empathy

put them to good work in the organization. This is one of the most important traits that the most successful servant leaders have used to serve their team.

To be able to learn this attribute of a servant leader, it is of importance that you strive with the desire to empathize with your employees. Everyone deserves a chance to be understood for who they are- their unique character traits, abilities, personal desires, etc. Try as often as possible to go out of your way to accept your team players as they are. However, taking your employees for who they are doesn't mean you should put up with certain characters and behavior that could disrupt the smooth running of the organization.

Listening

Servant leaders who have shown much willingness to listen and communicate with their followers are always valued. Paying close and rapt attention whenever your followers want to speak to you has a way of getting to them. They are able to get free with you and eventually open up their deepest secrets to you. The freedom followers have with you helps you to have a better understanding of all the personal, interpersonal, and intellectual issues they go through.

Leaders who serve their followers are quick to realize the importance of paying attention to suggestions and ideas made by team members. Lending an attentive ear enables leaders to be able to resolve any recurring conflicts, guide others through counselling, and finally, train them towards becoming experts and servant leaders themselves.

To become adept at listening to one's followers, there has to be a more substantial commitment than an ordinary leader would have. There has to be that dedication towards wanting to listen to understand others. Remember, it is only when you listen enough and learn to read the expressions of your followers that you can be said to be empathetic. So, learn to listen more and to judge others less. This is the only way you can learn to understand and be understood by your followers.

Awareness

So many leaders in places of position painfully fail to be conscious of their "self" as leaders. This is not the case for a servant leader who continually reflects on themselves. A servant leader understands perfectly what their strengths are, their weaknesses, abilities, qualities, values, and emotional status. It is the knowledge of these that he uses to their benefit, that is, growing their relationship with the workers as well as the organization. Laozi says, "He [she] who controls others may be powerful, but he who has mastered himself is mightier still[32]."

Now, the awareness of the self ensures that the servant leader understands their prejudices that might obstruct the

---

[32] https://www.brainyquote.com/quotes/lao_tzu_385970

discharge of their duties. He or she immediately sets them aside for more objective bases while making important decisions. The servant leader is open to learning from employees within the establishment who might have more knowledge about their field than anyone else. This openness and willingness to learn help to foster a learning and sharing of knowledge culture within the establishment. It then transcends to the growth and development of personal development and the organization.

Those who intend to learn this attribute of leadership should realize the need to understand themselves first. To be able to offer service to others in the best capacity, you will be derailed if you are unable to get rid of your biases. Socrates, the Greek philosopher, believed that man should always check himself, like the gadfly putting you on your toes. Learn to view every situation from an objective, holistic point. It is this burning awareness that puts a servant leader to work.

Healing

Most relationships out there require a lifeline, that is, healing of some sort. Healing is a potent force that can drive the transformation, mending, and merging of hearts alongside the integration of human existence. Servant leaders possess the attributes needed to help heal those who are emotionally down.

Emotional breakdowns, hurts, and broken spirits are a normal part of human existence. But it is not healthy emotionally, spiritually, and mentally to remain in such states. Servant leaders realize this is an opportunity to help and capitalize on their wealth of experience to solve everyone's emotional distraught. This, in turn, endears a servant leader to everyone because of their show of love, care, and support of their problems.

People immediately show faith to and trust to the leader for their efforts. Martin Luther King, Jr. says, "Everybody can be great…because anybody can serve. You don't have to have a college degree to serve. You don't have to make your subject and verb agree to serve. You only need a heart full of grace. A soul generated by love[33]."

Aspiring servant leaders should understand that every stated attribute of a leader is interwoven. It takes a leader who has excellent communication and empathy to understand and to find out what people are going through. Always try to find every means to put a smile on the faces of those around you when they are down emotionally. Show them love and understanding. It brings about a sense of belonging between the leader and those who surround them. Greenleaf mentions something related to this when he says, "There is something subtle communicated to one who is being served and led if, implicit in the compact

---

[33] https://www.goodreads.com/quotes/757-everybody-can-be-great-because-anybody-can-serve-you-don-t-have

between a servant leader and led, is the understanding that the search for wholeness is something they share[34]."

Conceptualization

A servant leader through conceptualization can think beyond the present problems that an organization faces. Changes cannot materialize if one does not think outside the box or beyond the present day to day activities. A famous wise saying says, "It is only a fool who does the same thing the same way and expects a different result[35]." Servant leaders know the implications of sitting down without searching for ways to turn difficult situations around into success stories.

Conceptualization requires zeal, determination, discipline, grit and constant practice to perfect or achieve. Servant leaders try everything within their mental capacity to look beyond achieving present goals. On the other hand, traditional leaders are enamored with the prospects of attaining short-term goals. Those who aspire to become servant leaders should not tread on the same path of traditional leaders. They should instead base their thinking on broader or long-term conceptualization.

---

[34] https://www.spearscenter.org/46-uncategorised/136-ten-characteristics-of-servant-leadership

[35] https://www.brainyquote.com/quotes/unknown_133991

Finally, a servant leader should not place the entire basis of their leadership on the operation of the organization. Emphasis also has to be placed on the conceptual projections. Therefore, the servant leader should learn to bridge the gap between the day-to-day operations of workers and conceptual analysis of the organization.

Persuasion

The art of persuasion is vital in the servant leader's ability to influence the decisions of people. Servant leaders place more premium on learning how to persuade others to make favorable opinions and decisions. To them, it is more important to know how to persuade than to rely on the power of their position to get others to action. He or she is more interested in convincing others to understand the reasons for actions rather than resorting to coercion.

This attribute of a servant leader draws a clear line of distinction between it and a traditional leadership attribute. The servant leader cares more about their abilities to help their organization negotiate with their business partners, government personnel, customers, etc. It is this power of persuasion he or she transfers to cater for the welfare of those around him, going on to influence their lives positively.

Learning this leadership attribute for those who want to become servant leaders does not come easy. It is advised that constant practice be made every day to perfect the persuasion attribute. Why is that so? Because you don't want to come off as being unnatural, thereby leading to the loss of respect and distrust for you among your peers.

Stewardship

A servant leader acts in the role of a steward who helps to oversee the resources of an organization. A steward is a person who manages the property or affairs of another entity. In this case, the servant leader is the steward in charge of the management of the existing resources pool of an organization for the mutual benefits and good fortune of all.

Servant leaders shoulder the task or responsibility of the whole organization, putting aside selfish interest. The focal point of their association with the management and employees is to serve them in every possible way he can. He or she is something similar to the Utilitarian who looks out for the common good of the establishment and its staff.

Understanding the principle surrounding stewardship allows one to become a better servant leader. People tend to look up to those who show exemplary leadership, just like the servant leader does. Shelve aside every iota of egoism while learning to become a servant leader. Servant leaders are altruistic, and you should become one if you indeed want to master the qualities of a servant leader.

Nelson Mandela says, "It is better to lead from behind and to put others in front, especially when you celebrate victory when nice things occur. You take the front line when there is danger. Then people will appreciate your leadership[36]." People realize the leadership traits you have when you show qualities of your being a leader.

Foresight

Servant leaders possess the ability to tell what the future might look like intuitively. Foresight is an ability that distinguishes any leader from an ordinary person who just takes what the day brings for him. Everything within space and time seems to be connected one way or another. From the past to the present to the future, a connectedness exists. Servant leaders understand this principle, and like those who learn from history, they sum up the past and present and tell the possibilities of the future.

Servant leaders are known for their excellent visionary techniques. Since they know the past and present, they try to plan to achieve desired results in the future. They make these plans in line with their predictions for the future.

To master servant leadership, it is pertinent that one learns this attribute, too. What is the essence of being just a leader who cares for the people alone if he cannot proffer solutions to crucial

---

[36] https://www.brainyquote.com/quotes/nelson_mandela_393048

problems that ail the people or the organization? Take this as a note to guide you while learning to become a servant leader.

Community building

Servant leaders understand the need for the creation of a community for those who have come together for the same aim. The servant leader makes everyone feel their impact on the development of the community. Although the community is larger than the individual, keeping the community compact means each individual has to feel accepted within the community.

Servant leaders lead with an exemplary lifestyle to every individual within the created community. He or she is very aware that humans are displaced by the creation of larger institutions as opposed to smaller units of the past. To make sure that the people experience togetherness in the new community, he or she preaches oneness. They make sure their love and care for every individual is known to all within the community this makes the individuals work in tandem as a team.

Robert Greenleaf made a statement that corroborates with the servant leader's aim mentioned above. He says, "All that is needed to rebuild community as a viable life form for large numbers of people is for enough servant-leaders to show the way, not by mass movements, but by each servant-leader demonstrating their or her unlimited liability for a quite specific community-related group[37]."

Commitment to the growth of others

Servant leaders believe they should always shoulder the responsibility of developing others. For them, every human has an intrinsic value within themselves waiting for it to be developed. This intrinsic value goes beyond the mere contributions workers make at their workplace. This is why servant leaders spend most of their time immersing themselves in training their workers. Clayton Christensen says, "my conclusion: Management is the most noble of professions if it's practiced well. No other occupation offers as many ways to help others learn and grow, take responsibility and be recognized for achievement, and contribute to the success of a team[38]."

The training that a servant leader gives to workers is not meant for the organization's growth alone. It is also to the end of workers growing and developing in their career paths, personal life, intellectually, etc. This is why servant leaders encourage workers to share their ideas in the decision-making process for the management of the organization. They give them all the encouragement they need to become better than they are within

---

37 https://the16percent.com/2014/06/18/the-servant-leader-and-building-community/
38 https://hbr.org/2017/08/how-new-managers-can-send-the-right-leadership-signals

the workplace and when they finally leave there (for greener pastures).

Patience, faith, and perseverance

If there is one thing that is constant in the experience of leadership, then it is that of change. With change come difficulties, pains, joy, smiles, and so on (whatever may be the case) in the course of leadership. Change is an important event or tool servant leaders need to understand to manipulate situations in their favor. A thing does not change from what it is to become something else in a blink of an eye; it takes time. It takes only the patient to make changes they want.

Servant leaders have to realize that for their dreams and visions for the people or organization to materialize, it does not come easy. When things don't come easy, it is not time to give up on the dream. Instead, it is time to exercise patience, perseverance, and muster enough zeal to achieve the goals at hand.

Servant leaders must possess the virtue of patience to persevere whenever decisions backfire. There must be that level of willingness to keep on trying, to wait till results become positive. Servant leaders after setting out attainable goals for the management only need to look forward. They need to look towards the destination and not the beginning where they started. Look forward until you reach the climax of success.

Life is not a bed of roses. Only those who are tough can patiently wait and persevere to the fruition of their desires. You would not want to set a bad example for your followers to copy. Remember, followers tend to look towards their leaders for encouragement, courage, and final go-ahead before making decisions. They become less motivated to carry out tasks once they realize that you always give up on decisions easily. This is why, as a servant leader, you don't need to take rash and quick decisions unless the situation demands it. You need to set out for yourself goals and plans that can be achievable. Doing this is enough motivation for you to keep on working towards the set goal, even if it doesn't work out in the first place.

Finally, remember to always exercise faith within yourself that the best will come out of your decisions. The possession of belief is what differentiates a successful person from the unsuccessful. It is the positive energy you get from belief that can allow you to maintain your patience and equally persevere. This positive vibe quickly spreads from a leader to team players once they notice it exhibited.

Selflessness

The defining feature or attribute of a servant leader is selflessness. In the first instance, there is nothing like being a servant leader without selflessness. A servant leader is called to serve, and that is what selflessness is about! Service to the people!

As a servant leader or one in the process, you need to understand that the people come first in every situation. They are the reason why you were placed in a leadership position in the first place. Always be willing to make sacrifices for your employees at every given opportunity. This genuine charismatic act of selflessness rubs off on their minds, causing them to remain loyal and under your influence. Never forget to do this every day.

Final notes on servant leadership

We all cannot underestimate the powers and influence that comes with the practice of servant leadership. Servant leadership allows you to have a great impact on people to do things for you without necessarily coercing them to do so. This is the power of influence!

Ken Blanchard says, "the key to successful leadership today is influence, not authority[39]." You don't necessarily have to flex your muscles to show you are the strongest man or women in the battle ring. Men of intellect know better than to rely on their physical or positional capacities to control others to do their bidding. This is just as servant leadership offers character traits with which you can easily influence people around you with charisma.

The servant leadership attributes/steps give leeway with which you can gain the support of those who follow you without

---

39 https://www.brainyquote.com/quotes/ken_blanchard_307860

appearing fake or deceitful. Learning them will make everything you do come out natural because it is a part of you that you imbibe through hard work and dedication.

Practice the different attributes given as steps, one for each month. Within them lies the key to making you fulfill your potential of being the leader people want!

Conclusion

The benefits of servant leadership to influencing one's followers to become loyalists cannot be overstated. Great leaders in the past and present have been able to learn the all-important lesson that their followers need to be prioritized first. This is a new knowledge that should be tapped by those who are new or exhibit potentials of leadership.

Followers feel secure around leaders who show them care, love, and understanding because this builds them to overcome any circumstance. Creating an atmosphere of followers first in one's workplace or society has multiple ripple effects on the people. People are made to be more productive, budding servant leaders, team workers, and many more. This is the secret of the greatest leaders who exist or have existed in the world.

Each chapter given within the book attempts to break down servant leadership to ways to practice becoming a servant leader. Consideration was made on what traditional leadership can do to cost leaders who show potentials of leadership their abilities to influence the people. It's easy to get influence by the position of power we occupy, but it is best to grow out of this leadership style. Choose instead to pitch your tent with becoming a servant leader.

The different steps towards becoming a servant leader should be taken one at a time. There is no need to rush them all in one fell swoop, so you don't become confused and lose focus. Take your time and see the changes that occur in your leadership profile.

ABOUT THE AUTHOR

Danny Doucette, MBA, MPA, is a Certified Life Coach and Executive Coach with over 12 years of Leadership consultant. Danny has coached leaders within the government service, including Army, Air Force, Navy, Marines, and Coast Guard. He has partnered with several universities and colleges and taught Organization Behavior for 12 years and continues as a consultant in many of these universities and colleges.

His Bachelor of Science in Criminal Justice, MBA in Management, and MPA in Human Resources make him highly qualified to coach in organizational behavior at the C-suite level. He is an Associate Certified Coach (ACC) from the largest International Coaching Federation organization in the world.

Additionally, he's a retired law enforcement police officer with the New York City Police Department and has served during the attacks of September 11th, 2001. As a former Chief Academic Officer of an Academy, he is highly qualified in leading teams of teams and enjoys training and development of clients.

Danny is passionate about teaching organizational behavior, leadership, and resiliency to government and business clients. His moving 9/11 stories of resiliency have been widely heard thousands of times and requested by clients hundreds of times.

Danny is a servant leader who enjoys coaching clients from all around the world.

https://www.linkedin.com/in/danny-doucette-mba-mpa-icf-acc-certified-coach-904a07126/

Made in United States
Orlando, FL
20 March 2024